Pearls Before Swine

BLTs Taste So Darn Good

by Stephan Pastis

Andrews McMeel
Publishing

Kansas City

Pearls Before Swine is distributed internationally by United Feature Syndicate.

Pearls Before Swine copyright © 2003 by Stephan Pastis. All rights reserved. Printed in the United States of America. No part of this book may be used or reproduced in any manner whatsoever without written permission except in the case of reprints in the context of reviews. For information, write Andrews McMeel Publishing,LLC, an Andrews McMeel Universal company, 4520 Main Street, Kansas City, Missouri 64111.

07 08 09 BBG 12 1110

ISBN-13: 978-0-7407-3437-3
ISBN-10: 0-7407-3437-7

Library of Congress Control Number: 2002111890

Pearls Before Swine can be viewed on the Internet at:

www.comics.com/comics/pearls

These strips appeared in newspapers 12/31/01 - 10/6/02

———— **ATTENTION: SCHOOLS AND BUSINESSES** ————

Andrews McMeel books are available at quantity discounts with bulk purchase for educational, business, or sales promotional use. For information, please write to: Special Sales Department, Andrews McMeel Publishing, LLC, 4520 Main Street, Kansas City, Missouri 64111

Pearls Before Swine

For Staci,

For my mom and dad,

And for every lawyer who ever dreamed of quitting his day job.

Introduction

In the summer of 1999, comic strip syndicates were all about demographics. A new strip had to have a specific target audience in mind—young girls, retired people, soccer moms, it didn't really matter. It just had to have a set demographic to be marketable. And better yet, syndicates preferred that the cartoonist have an established name, such as someone who already had another strip going, or someone who was an editorial cartoonist for some newspaper.

In the summer of 1999, I submitted a comic strip to the syndicates that had a nameless rat and pig who did not move, showed no expression, and discussed death in a majority of the strips. . . .

Find *that* demographic.

Making matters worse, I was a full-time lawyer. I had never sold a single cartoon to any publication in my life. The odds of even a safe strip achieving syndication are astronomical. Syndicates receive around 6,000 submissions a year, and out of those, they pick just two or three for possible syndication. Put this all together and you will find that the odds of *Pearls* succeeding were about 45 million to one.

So, you may ask, how in the world did this ever happen? Well, it happened because of other people.

It started with an editor at United Media named Amy Lago. There were other editors at other syndicates who were interested in *Pearls*, but they couldn't convince their sales staff that it was marketable. One syndicate would agree to syndicate it only if I eliminated Rat, the main character. By contrast, Amy would not give up on the strip, and she never asked me to make a single change to its content. In tandem with United's Web department—to whom I also owe a great debt—Amy got *Pearls* launched on their Web site (www.comics.com) to see what type of interest it generated. That happened in November 2000.

Reaction to the strip was strong, but not strong enough. Once again, the strip needed help from someone else. That someone else was Scott Adams, creator of *Dilbert*, who, unbeknownst to me at the time, was a fan of the strip. Just a few days before Christmas 2000, Scott gave me the greatest Christmas gift I'd ever received when he endorsed *Pearls* to all of his fans. Interest in the strip skyrocketed overnight and *Pearls* was on its way with a huge base of dedicated Web fans who were loyal and constant supporters of the strip.

But still, I was not out of the woods. I was, after all, a lawyer. I knew nothing about the technical aspects of cartooning. I couldn't add the shading to the daily strips and had no way of knowing how to color the Sunday strips. Once again, someone else stepped in. This time it was Darby Conley, creator of *Get Fuzzy*. Like an older brother, Darby took me under his wing from the very beginning and walked me through every step in the process. I don't know how I would have made it to this point without him.

But no one is more responsible for *Pearls* than my wife, Staci. Staci saw me through every step in the long history of *Pearls*. She did whatever was necessary to make sure I had the time and space to work on the strip, which is not an easy task, particularly when you have two young children. She took care of every detail, ran every errand. She put up with every one of my moods and saw me through every high and every low. For all of that, she is as much a part of *Pearls* as I am.

Someone once asked jazz trumpeter Dizzy Gillespie what fellow jazz great Louis Armstrong meant to him and his career. Gillespie responded simply, "No him, no me."

Well, I think that applies here. . . .

No them, no me.

—Stephan Pastis, March 2003

9

1/6

13

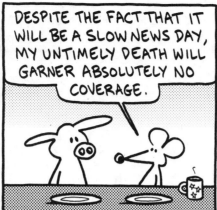

15

16

1/20

17

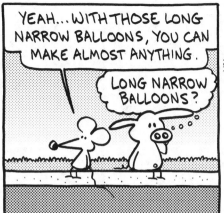

20

THE BEST PART ABOUT EATING AT A CHINESE RESTAURANT IS THE FORTUNE COOKIE AT THE END.

NOT FOR ME... I'M ALWAYS AFRAID I'LL GET A BAD ONE.

THAT'S RIDICULOUS... LOOK AT MINE... "FORTUNE WILL SMILE HER SWEET SMILE UPON YOU."

HEH HEH

HOW ABOUT YOURS?

"FORTUNE WILL SPIT IN YOUR EYE, YOU DUMB PIG."

MAYBE WE SHOULD EAT ITALIAN NEXT TIME.

 DEAR LIONS,
AS YOU MAY HAVE ASCER-
TAINED FROM OUR PRIOR
CORRESPONDENCE, WE
ZEBRAS ARE NOT PLEASED
WITH OUR RELATIONSHIP.

 WHILE WE RECOGNIZE AND
RESPECT NATURE'S LAW, WE
FEEL IT IS TIME TO MOVE
TOWARD A HIGHER STATE
OF CIVILIZATION....

 ...ONE IN WHICH THERE
EXISTS A MUTUAL RESPECT
FOR ONE ANOTHER'S NEEDS
AND DIFFERENCES.

 PLEASE FEEL FREE TO
CONTINUE THIS DIALOGUE
WITH SOME THOUGHTS
OF YOUR OWN.

 WE EAT YOU.

 SIGH...

26

27

29

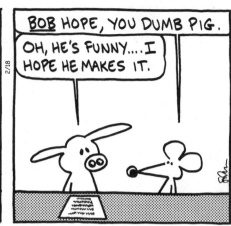

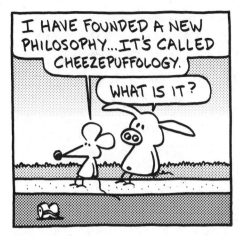

31

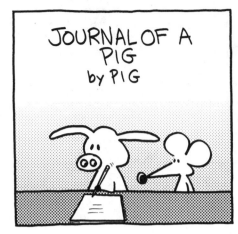

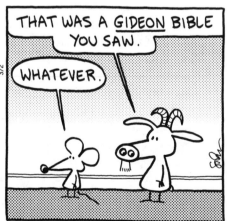

REMEMBER THAT OLD COMMERCIAL WITH THE INDIAN STANDING ON THE HIGHWAY WITH ONE TEAR ROLLING SLOWLY DOWN HIS FACE?

YEAH...THAT COMMERCIAL MADE A LOT OF PEOPLE THINK TWICE ABOUT LITTERING.

LITTERING? WHY DID IT MAKE THEM THINK ABOUT LITTERING?

BECAUSE THAT'S WHAT MADE THE INDIAN CRY.

OH....I THOUGHT SOMEONE RAN OVER HIS DOG.

I ALWAYS THOUGHT IT WAS MEAN TO THROW TRASH AT A GUY WHO'S JUST LOST HIS DOG.

36

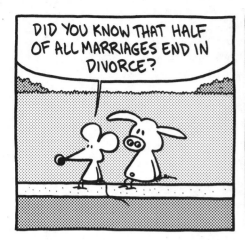

DEAR ANTELOPES,
GIVEN THE FACT THAT BOTH OF OUR HERDS ARE PURSUED BY THE DESPOTIC LIONS, WE HAVE AN OBVIOUS COMMONALITY OF INTEREST.

WE PROPOSE JOINTLY WRITING A BOOK FOR DISTRIBUTION AMONGST THE LIONS THAT WOULD PERSUADE THEM TO STOP PURSUING OUR RESPECTIVE HERDS.

ENCLOSED PLEASE FIND OUR PROPOSED CHAPTER ONE, TITLED, "WHY KILLING IS MORALLY WRONG."

WE WOULD GREATLY APPRECIATE IT IF YOU WOULD CONTRIBUTE A CHAPTER OF YOUR OWN.....

DEAR ZEBRAS,
ENCLOSED PLEASE FIND CHAPTER TWO, "FIFTY WAYS TO BARBECUE A ZEBRA."

45

48

49

50

4/14

YOU SAID THIS WAS BARRY BONDS' 74TH HOME-RUN BALL FROM LAST SEASON, BUT GOAT SAYS HE DIDN'T HIT 74, SO I WANT MY MONEY BACK.

GOSH... I THINK GOAT'S RIGHT... THIS APPEARS TO BE THE 75TH HOME-RUN BALL.... I'M GONNA HAVE TO CHARGE YOU A LOT MORE MONEY.

4/18

DO YOU TAKE CHECKS?

DEAR FIDEL CASTRO, HOW COME YOU WEAR THAT SAME GREEN UNIFORM ALL THE TIME? IT LOOKS KIND OF DUMB.

YOU STUPID PIG, WHY DO YOU BOTHER WRITING LETTERS LIKE THAT? NO ONE CARES WHAT YOU THINK........

4/19

WHAT ARE YOU READING?

"THE DECLINE AND FALL OF THE ROMAN EMPIRE."

4/20

NOT A LOT OF SUSPENSE WITH THAT ONE.

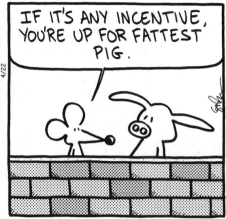

MY ZEBRA HERD IS NOW TRYING TO FOOL THE LIONS BY PLAYING DEAD.

DOES IT WORK?

STUDIES SHOW THAT NINETY-NINE OF THE HUNDRED ZEBRAS THAT TRIED IT WERE KILLED BY THE LIONS.

4/25

WHY DO THEY KEEP DOING IT?

THEY CAN'T READ.

DID YOU KNOW THAT FEMALE ELEPHANTS ARE CALLED COWS?

YOU MEAN THOSE THINGS WE GET MILK FROM ARE ACTUALLY ELEPHANTS?

NO. THOSE ARE COWS.

4/26

I UNDERSTAND. BUT IT'S STRANGE TO THINK THEY'RE REALLY ELEPHANTS.

WHAT ARE YOU WRITING?

A BOOK ON DINING ETIQUETTE.

IT'S FOR GUYS LIKE ME THAT HAVE TROUBLE RE-MEMBERING SOME OF THE MORE ESOTERIC RULES.

WHAT HAVE YOU GOT SO FAR?

4/27

"DON'T PUNCH YOUR DINNER GUESTS IN THE HEAD."

EVERYBODY SAYS YOU SHOULDN'T BE JUDGMENTAL, BUT HOW CAN YOU HELP IT WHEN LIFE IS FILLED WITH SO MANY IDIOTS?

THUS, I WILL NOW WEAR A BAG AND EARPLUGS.

WHAT WILL THAT DO?

WELL, IF I CAN'T SEE THE MORONS, I CAN'T JUDGE THE STUPID THINGS THEY DO......

...AND IF I CAN'T HEAR THE MORONS, I CAN'T JUDGE THE STUPID THINGS THEY SAY.

4/28

YOU SMELL.

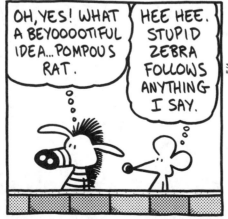

61

63

5/12

66

WHY DO THEY FILM THESE COMEDIES BEFORE A LIVE STUDIO AUDIENCE?

BECAUSE THEY TEST-MARKETED THE SHOW ON DEAD GUYS AND FOUND THEY NEVER LAUGHED.

5/16

TEST-MARKETING IS SO IMPORTANT.

WHAT ARE YOU WRITING?

A LIST OF THE THREE THINGS I'D ASK FOR IF I MET A GENIE.

THAT'S EASY FOR ME...LOVE, LOVE AND MORE LOVE. HOW ABOUT YOU?

UH.... MONEY, MONEY AND MORE MONEY.

5/17

I'LL BUY THE LOVE.

I MET A NICE GUY AT THE PARK TODAY.

WHAT WAS NICE ABOUT HIM?

HE'S THE ONLY PERSON I'VE EVER MET WHO JUST LISTENED TO EVERYTHING I SAID AND DIDN'T SAY ANYTHING MEAN OR RUDE IN RESPONSE.

5/18

ON THE DOWN SIDE, HE KEPT GETTING TRAPPED BEHIND AN INVISIBLE WALL.

69

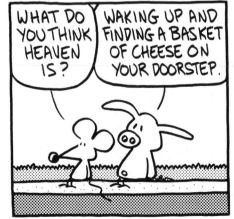

70

WHAT ARE YOU WATCHING?

SOME GUY THAT CLAIMS TO BE A SPIRITUAL MEDIUM.

WHAT'S THE GUY DO?

PEOPLE PAY HIM TONS OF CASH SO THEY CAN TALK TO THEIR DEAD RELATIVES.

5/27

GOSH... I DON'T EVEN WANT TO TALK TO MY LIVING ONES.

AND SO THE GUY SAYS, "SORRY, SIR, ALL PASSENGER CARRY-ON ITEMS MUST GO THROUGH THE X-RAY MACHINE..."

WHAT'D YOU DO?

I GRABBED MY SUITCASE WITH BOTH HANDS AND GAVE A BIG SPEECH ABOUT HOW SAD IT IS THAT NO ONE CAN TRUST ANYONE ANY MORE.

THEN WHAT?

5/28

...THAT'S WHEN THE SUITCASE BUSTED OPEN AND THE SIX HUNDRED CUBAN CIGARS ROLLED OUT.

I'VE JUST JOINED THIS PIG GROUP DEDICATED TO ELIMINATING PIG-BASED INSULTS FROM OUR EVERYDAY LANGUAGE.

LIKE WHAT?

WE'RE GONNA START WITH "COMMIE PIG." IT'S VERY DEROGATORY TOWARD PIGS.

WHAT ARE YOU PROPOSING PEOPLE SAY INSTEAD?

5/29

"COMMIE COW."

WHAT ARE YOU READING?

THIS BOOK ON HOW TO ACHIEVE FINANCIAL INDEPENDENCE.

HOW MUCH WAS IT?

5/30

I RIPPED IT OFF.

GOOD START.

DEAR JULIA ROBERTS, YOU ARE SO PRETTY AND SO SMART. I AM SO DUMB AND SO FAT.

I GUESS WHEN GOD WAS HANDING OUT THE GOOD STUFF, I MUSTA BEEN TAKING A POTTY BREAK.

5/31

WHAT A BEAUTIFUL IMAGE.

THANKS. IT'S HOW MY MOM EXPLAINED IT TO ME.

WHAT ARE YOU WATCHING?

SOME NATURE SHOW......

THIS FEMALE ELEPHANT IS LOOKING FOR A BULL TO MATE WITH.

6/1

THAT'S ONE KINKY ELEPHANT.

WHAT ARE YOU LOOKING AT?

JUST SOME COFFEE TABLE BOOK.

COFFEE TABLES? I JUST SEE PRETTY PICTURES OF FARMS.

IT'S THE ENGLISH COUNTRYSIDE.

6/2

WHERE ARE THE COFFEE TABLES?

THERE ARE NO COFFEE TABLES.

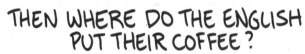

THEN WHERE DO THE ENGLISH PUT THEIR COFFEE?

YOU DUMB PIG!! IT'S NOT A BOOK ABOUT COFFEE TABLES..... IT'S A BOOK ABOUT THE ENGLISH COUNTRYSIDE!! CAN'T YOU GET THAT THROUGH YOUR THICK HEAD?!?

MAYBE THAT'S WHY THEY DRINK TEA INSTEAD.

75

78

82

84

6/30

MY MOM IS AN OX.

WHAT?

LOOK...SHE SIGNED HER LETTER "MOM OX."

SHE'S GIVING YOU HUGS AND KISSES.

I DON'T WANT THEM FROM AN OX.

CAN I HELP YOU, SIR?

YEAH, I JUST PUT MY A.T.M. CARD IN YOUR A.T.M. OUTSIDE AND I CAN'T GET IT BACK.

FIRST NATIONAL BANK OF PASTIS

WE DON'T HAVE AN A.T.M.

WHAT'S THAT OUT FRONT?

A NEWSPAPER RACK.

FIRST NATIONAL BANK OF PASTIS

....CAN I BORROW A QUARTER?

FIRST NATIONAL BANK OF PASTIS

TELEVISION IS CLEARLY THE MOST IMPORTANT DEVELOPMENT OF THE TWENTIETH CENTURY.

WHAT ABOUT THE POLIO VACCINE? THAT WAS KIND OF IMPORTANT.

NOT TO ME, IT ISN'T.... I DON'T HAVE POLIO.

89

I HEARD YOU'RE DRAWING A COMIC STRIP THAT IS A RIP-OFF OF "DILBERT."

OH, I SEE... JUST BECAUSE I DO A STRIP ABOUT AN OFFICE WORKER NAMED "BILDERT", I'M RIPPING SOMEONE OFF, HUH?

THE TIE THAT CURLS UPWARD IS ANOTHER HINT.

PLEASE... IT'S WINDY WHERE BILDERT LIVES.

WHAT'D YOU BUY?

A COLLECTION OF LAST YEAR'S "DILBERT" STRIPS.

BOOKS

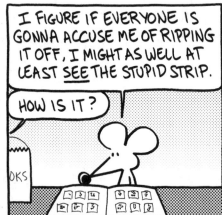

I FIGURE IF EVERYONE IS GONNA ACCUSE ME OF RIPPING IT OFF, I MIGHT AS WELL AT LEAST SEE THE STUPID STRIP.

HOW IS IT?

BORING..... DID I MENTION I RECENTLY HAD ABOUT 365 NEW IDEAS FOR MY BILDERT STRIP?

BOOKS

MY BILDERT STRIP HAS IMPROVED SINCE MY INTRODUCTION OF THE PRICKLY-HAIRED BOSS.

THAT LOOKS EXACTLY LIKE DILBERT'S BOSS.

PLEASE. DILBERT'S BOSS'S HAIR STICKS UP AT A NINETY DEGREE ANGLE FROM THE TOP OF HIS HEAD... THE HAIR ON BILDERT'S BOSS IS AT AN OBVIOUS SEVENTY-EIGHT DEGREE ANGLE.

....YOU NEED TO THINK BEFORE YOU TALK.

SORRY... I LEFT MY PROTRACTOR AT HOME.

Panel 1: "GOAT SAYS YOUR BILDERT STRIP IS A BLATANT RIP-OFF OF 'DILBERT.'"

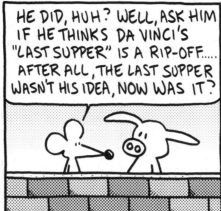

Panel 2: "HE DID, HUH? WELL, ASK HIM IF HE THINKS DA VINCI'S 'LAST SUPPER' IS A RIP-OFF..... AFTER ALL, THE LAST SUPPER WASN'T HIS IDEA, NOW WAS IT?"

7/11

Panel 3: "YOU'RE A GOOD DEBATER."

Panel 4: "SCOTT ADAMS IS SUING ME...... HE SAYS MY BILDERT STRIP IS A COMPLETE RIP-OFF OF HIS 'DILBERT' STRIP."

Panel 5: "WHAT ARE YOU GONNA DO?"
"FIND A LAWYER WHO'LL RECOGNIZE THE OBVIOUS DIFFERENCES AND DEFEND ME."

7/12

Panel 6: "DILBERT: FIVE LUMPS OF HAIR."
"BILDERT: NO MORE THAN FOUR."

Panel 7: "THIS BOOK I'M READING SAYS THAT WHEN A MAN GETS MARRIED, HIS LIFE IS OVER.... HOWEVER, MOST MEN WILL NOT ACKNOWLEDGE THAT FACT."
"OH."

Panel 8: "INSTEAD, THEY ENTER A STAGE OF DENIAL WHERE THEY TRY TO CONVINCE THEMSELVES AND OTHERS THAT THEY REMAIN FREE, VIRILE BEINGS."
"WHEN DOES THAT END?"

7/13

Panel 9: "WHEN THEY BUY THEIR FIRST MINI-VAN.....THEN THE GIG IS UP."

HOW'S YOUR EFFORT GOING TO PROTECT YOUR FELLOW ZEBRAS FROM THE LIONS?

NOT GOOD...THE POPEMOBILES WERE A COMPLETE FIASCO.

POPEMOBILES?

YEAH....YOU KNOW THAT LITTLE BUBBLE CAR THE POPE RIDES IN?....EACH OF THE ZEBRAS BOUGHT ONE.

DID THEY WORK?

TOO WELL....AFTER AWHILE, NONE OF THE ZEBRAS WOULD GET OUT OF THEIR CARS AND THE WHOLE HERD DIED OFF.

BUT I THOUGHT THEY WERE PROTECTED.

THEY WERE.

BUT IT'S HARD TO MAKE BABIES BLOWING KISSES THROUGH WINDOWS.

7/14

92

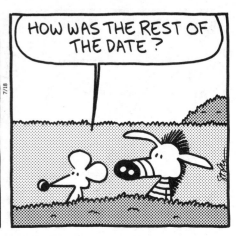

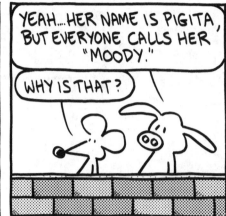

98

AND SO THE CROSSING GUARD LOOKS AT ME LIKE I'M SOME KIND OF PSYCHO AND SAYS, "YOU'LL STOP YOUR CAR WHEN I SAY SO."

SO I ROLL DOWN THE WINDOW AND YELL AT THE GUY, "LISTEN, MISTER, THIS IS JUST HOW THEM NAZIS IN CANADA GOT THEIR START."

7/29

GERMANY. AND I DON'T THINK THEY GOT THEIR START BEING SCHOOL CROSSING GUARDS.

SHOULDA SEEN THE LOOK ON THAT IDIOT'S FACE.

I'M STARTING MY OWN CELEBRITY TALK SHOW ON THE PUBLIC ACCESS CHANNEL.

WILL YOU HAVE GUESTS?

OF COURSE I'LL HAVE GUESTS... MAYBE NOT THE BIGGEST STARS AT FIRST, BUT I'LL WORK MY WAY UP TO IT......

7/30

SO, FRED, DO YOU ENJOY BEING MY GARBAGEMAN?

RAT, THE TALK SHOW HOST

MY FIRST GUEST TONIGHT IS MYRA HERTZ...SO, MYRA, WHAT'S YOUR LATEST FILM PROJECT?

NONE. I'M A WAITRESS AT "WAFFLE BARN." AND YOU KNOW THAT.

7/31

LET'S GIVE A BIG SHOUT-OUT TO WAFFLES.

RAT, THE TALK SHOW HOST

...NEXT WEEK ON THE SHOW, WE'LL HAVE LEGENDARY CROONER, BING CROSBY.

PSST PSST PSST

FOLKS, I'M AFRAID I HAVE SOME BAD NEWS.

THAT STUPID PUBLIC ACCESS CHANNEL CANCELED MY TALK SHOW AND REPLACED IT WITH SOME INSTRUCTIONAL SHOW ON CHEERLEADING.

CHEERLEADING?

YEAH, CAN YOU IMAGINE THAT? AS IF SOME MORON'S GONNA SIT IN HIS LIVING ROOM AND LEARN TO BE A CHEERLEADER.

PUSH 'EM BACK!! PUSH 'EM BACK!! WAAAAAAY BACK!!

SOME PEOPLE BELIEVE THAT AFTER YOU DIE, YOU RETURN TO LIFE IN A FORM BEFITTING THE TYPE OF LIFE YOU PRE-VIOUSLY LED.

I MUST HAVE BEEN REALLY BAD.

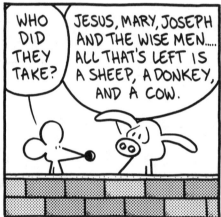

102

8/11

104

MY ZEBRA HERD HELD A "TUPPERWARE" PARTY TO TRY AND TAKE THEIR MINDS OFF THE LIONS.

HOW'D IT GO?

BAD....THE LIONS CRASHED IT AND FEASTED ON ALL THE ZEBRAS.

8/12

WELL AT LEAST THEY HAD SOMEWHERE TO PUT THEIR LEFTOVERS.

HERE ARE YOUR FRIED WONTONS, GENTLEMEN.

HEY BABY..... HOW 'BOUT A LITTLE ACTION?

SURE THING, SWEETIE..... MY PLATE OR YOURS?

8/13

I CAN'T STAND WANTON WONTONS.

I'LL HAVE THE SOUP DU JOUR.

FINE. SOUP OF THE DAY FOR YOU.

OH, NO... I DON'T WANT THE SOUP OF THE DAY.

THE SOUP OF THE DAY IS THE SOUP DU JOUR.

OH, GREAT... I THOUGHT IT WAS THAT LOUSY CLAM CHOWDER.

8/14

IT IS.

OH, GEEZ... THEN JUST GIVE ME THE SOUP DU JOUR.

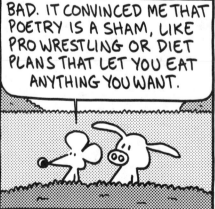

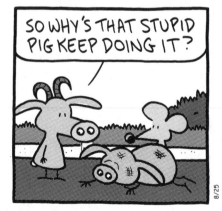

111

I'M GOING INTO THE SPORTING GOODS INDUSTRY.

WHAT FOR?

I FOUND A MARKET NEED.... SEE....ANYONE THAT WANTS TO PLAY FOOTBALL HAS ONLY ONE CHOICE...TO USE THIS...

WHAT'S WRONG WITH THAT?

BOOOOORING...PEOPLE WANT VARIETY IN THEIR FOOTBALLS...THUS, I'VE INVENTED THIS...

IT'S THE "BOB, THE ANGRY SMOKER FOOTBALL".....THE LIT CIGARETTE IS OPTIONAL, OF COURSE.

HOW ARE YOU SUPPOSED TO PLAY WITH THAT??

WELL, SPIRALS MAY BE HARD, BUT OTHER THAN THAT, IT'LL BE FINE.

9/1

WANNA TOSS IT AROUND?

SURE.

GO LONG GO LONG

I GOT IT I GOT IT

NUTS....IT GOT STUCK IN THAT TREE.

THAT'S OKAY... WE'LL GET IT TOMORROW.

WHAT DOES IT MEAN IF YOU ARE GIVEN SOMETHING POSTHUMOUSLY?

I THINK IT MEANS THEY KICK YOU IN THE REAR.

THAT'S "POSTERIOR".... "POSTHUMOUS" IS AFTER YOU DIE.

I'D HATE TO GET KICKED IN THE REAR AFTER I DIE.

WHEN ARE YOU GONNA GET THE BATHROOM DOOR FIXED? IT'S STILL STICKING.

BUT I KNOW NOTHING ABOUT CONSTRUCTION.

WHAT'S THERE TO KNOW? JUST PICK UP THE PHONE AND CALL A FIX-IT GUY.

SO WHAT WILL THIS ENTIRELY NEW FOUNDATION COST?

NO WAY TO TELL.... JUST SIGN BELOW.

I HEARD YOUR ZEBRA HERD HAS STARTED A "JOKES FOR LIFE" PROGRAM.

YEAH... WE GO TO THE CROCODILES AND TELL THEM JOKES...

WE BELIEVE THAT INTRODUCING HUMOR INTO THEIR LIVES MAY MAKE THEM MORE CIVILIZED AND LESS LIKELY TO KILL US.

WHAT ZEBRA SAY BEFORE I EAT HIM?

WHAT ZEBRA SAY?

WHO CARE? HE TASTE SO GUD.

HAHAHAHA HAHAHAHA

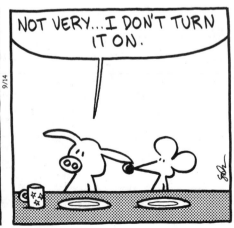

"The Adventures of Angry Bob" Volume I

by *Rat*

Angry Bob was angry. Very, very angry. He went to the Waffle Barn and ordered two waffles but they did not make him happy.

He went to the park. It was sunny. He sat on the warm grass and took off his shoes and smoked a cigarette. It felt good.

He spotted the hot dog man. "I will buy a hot dog and a lemonade and read a book," he said. "Then I will be happy."

Bob ate his hot dog and drank his lemonade. He put on his glasses and began to read his book. The happiness that had eluded Angry Bob for 33 years was finally his.

A Frisbee smashed into Bob's face. Bob choked on the hot dog and died.

THERE'S A LESSON IN THERE SOMEWHERE.

9/15

119

"The Adventures of Angry Bob" Volume II by *Rat*

Angry Bob undied.

To celebrate the miracle of Angry Bob, the pious townfolk ordered a sacrifice . . . The big, fat goat was the first to go.

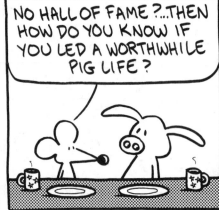

"The Adventures of Angry Bob" Volume III
by Rat

Angry Bob was angry. He went to the diner and punched Frank.

Frank punched Bob back. So Bob punched Frank. And Bob punched Frank.

And Bob punched Frank.
And Bob punched Frank.
And Bob punched Frank.

GEEZ, ALL THIS FIGHTING....IF YOU'RE GONNA SELL THIS NOVEL TO WOMEN, YOU'RE GONNA NEED A LITTLE ROMANCE IN THERE TOO.

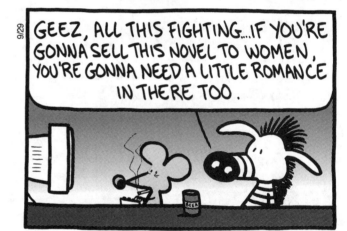

Myra smiled at Bob.
Bob smiled at Myra.
And Bob punched Frank.

126

Dear Mr. Publisher,
I recently received a form letter from you saying that you had rejected my manuscript, "The Adventures of Angry Bob."

As a professional myself, I realize that you have a job to do and have to make close judgment calls like this on a daily basis. Thus, I am not one to whine.

At the same time, I am sure we both realize on a gut level that "Angry Bob" could revolutionize publishing.

TYPE TYPE TYPE

For now, why don't you share with me your thought process in this regard and let us see what we can do to move this project forward

10/6

Dear Sir,
You are the worst writer I have seen in 46 years in the publishing business. May a bus run you over.

THESE PERSONALIZED REJECTIONS ARE A GREAT SIGN.